Mœris
and the Secret Dollar
Ligature Œ

Includes the mandala of infinite abundance and prosperity

Jorge A. Rodríguez
(JAR)

Text and illustrations

Text and illustrations: Jorge A. Rodríguez (JAR)
©2015 Jorge A. Rodríguez (JAR) All rights reserved.
ISBN-13: 978-1522866190
ISBN-10: 1522866191
E-mail: jarrodriguezve@gmail.com
Facebook: Jorge A. Rodriguez Jar
Twitter: @jar_rodriguez

My best wishes *vœux*
to all of those
who from the heart *cœur*
read this work *œuvre*
and
also to those who
only give it
a glance *un coup d'œil*

JAR

Mœris wants to be a successful businessman. One morning very early ... - *"**Mœris**: secret and action, it's in your name"* - listened, almost awakening, with the first light of day entering through an oval window (an ox-eye window) **œil de bœuf**, illuminating a dollar bill.

Mœris internet searches French words that are written with the ligature **œ**, given that, in his name, is the only thing that he sees different.

His first company will sell some food products that, in French, are written with the ligature **œ**, therefore have in mind that phrase ... *"**Mœris**: secret and action, it's in your name."*

Its menu includes eggs **œufs**, tomatoes "ox heart" **"cœur de bœuf"**, ox eyes **"œil de bœuf"**, coelacanth **cœlacanthes** fish, all arranged as appetizers **hors d' œuvres**, and also some old enology **œnologie** books, that he ordered heart **cœur** shaped...

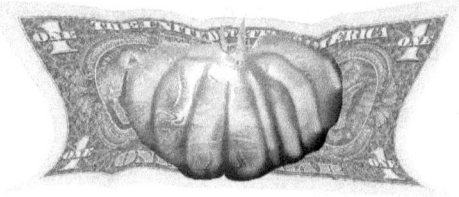

Hours later, the sale was a total failure, caused disgust and revulsion **écœurante**.

Mœris disappointed, wonders-what is failing? - ... *"**Mœris**: secret and action, it's in your name"*...

Mœris thinks and stares at his name ... the ligature **œ** ... "That's it! ... Everything is linked, fused. I will make an energy shake with all this," said **Mœris**- And prepared an energy shake with all these snacks **hors d' œuvres**. The eggs **œufs**, ox eyes **œil de bœuf**, tomatoes "ox heart" **"cœur de bœuf'**, and many coelacanth **cœlacanthe** fish eggs **œufs**.

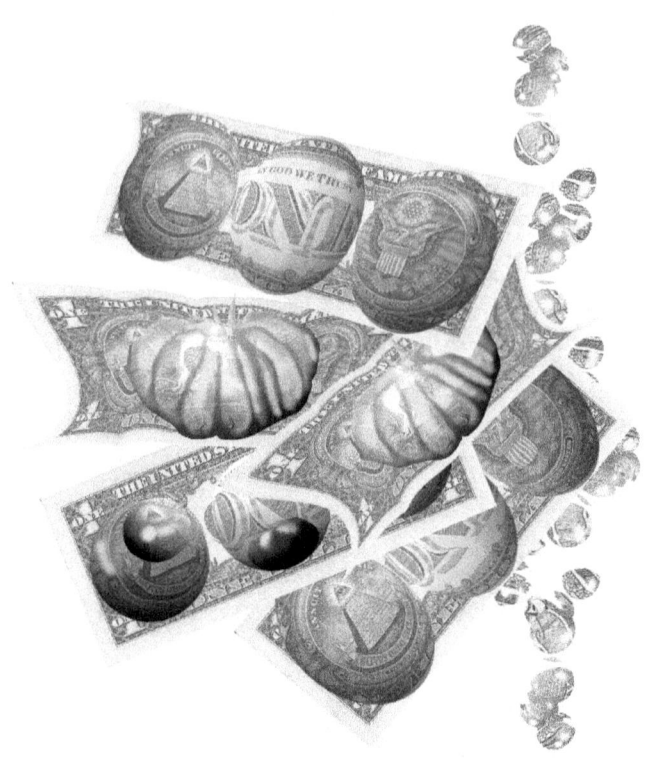

Again his company was a total failure, caused disgust and revulsion **écœurante. Mœris**, disappointed, sees himself as a loser unemployed **désœuvré. Mœris**, totally disgusted **écœuré**, filled with rancor **rancœur**, eats everything in which he had invested time and money...

Mœris was admitted to a clinic for severe irritation of the esophagus **œsophage**. Already in the clinic, **Mœris** explains to his father and little sister **sœurette Clœlia**, what he wanted to do and what his intentions as an entrepreneur were.

"**Mœris**, you are very creative and intelligent, but you were very greedy and selfish. If you want to be a successful businessman, and want **vœux** to multiply your money, you need to learn to share and let rancor **rancœur**" wisely said his little sister **sœurette Clœlia** winking an eye **clin d'œil**.-

At dusk, Already at home and before bedtime, **Mœris** carefully observed a dollar bill, like one who meditates observing a mandala, until he fell asleep in fetal **fœtal** position...

In the ligature œ, the "o" and "e" share the same space, give each of himself and create a new identity: the ligature œ. The Self is in Alchemy creation of the Great Work **Œuvre**, where opposites fused, without polarity... *"**Mœris**: secret and action, it's in your name"* he recalled those words in his sleep-

Mœris sees himself immersed in the back of the dollar, goes up the pyramid and reaches the eye **œil** of providence, the eye **œil** that sees everything, and on it he reads the Latin words **"ANNUIT CŒPTIS"** "OUR COMPANY IS SUCCESSFUL" also translated as: "GOD FAVORED OUR COMPANY".

Mœris, like on a skateboard, powered by a ray of golden light, jumps from letter to letter, performing risky maneuvers **manœuvres** and when he reached letter number eight: the ligature **Œ**, starts making twists and turns on it drawing number eight, infinity symbol and abundance, an eight that flows in a continuous motion, as the moebius strip **ruban de mœbius**, where opposite fused, without polarity. The moebius strip **ruban de mœbius** is a unity, a limitless totality, without opposites, where giving and receiving is the same, a flow of generosity and infinite abundance.

In his dream, jumps from the ligature **Œ** to the center of the pyramid, passing by the eye and down in a diagonal... goes above the "N" of "NOVUS ORDO SECLORUM" (A NEW ORDER OF THE AGES) and continues down until arriving just in the center, on the basis of the "N" (of ONE), and continues to the corner of the dollar bill, rushing to the void and suddenly waking up with a feeling of angst...

Awake, **Mœris** draw a line from the ligature **œ** that is in the Latin words **"ANNUIT CŒPTIS"** to the "N" of "ONE" on left lower side of the dollar and relates the fact that reaches the corner, with "folding" the corner: and begins to fold the dollar bill, the first of many possible ways… until he folds it in the upper left corner, lowering it and forming a triangle, right up to the limit of the "I" of "IN GOD WE TRUST"

Then folds the bill from the "E" of big "ONE", to the left, and carries it carefully until the first fold, until completely hide the words "IN GOD WE TRUST".

Mœris considers, and finds that, the stop seeing these words, there has been an act of faith. We must remember what the eye **œil** doesn't see. And that's where as in a magic act, lifting the triangular fold which is on the left, appears the ligature **Œ** that has always been there.

Thus, the slogan announcing the Eagle Great Seal is accomplished (Bird **Phœnix**, in the proposal of the original Barton-Thomson design, 1782) "E PLURIBUS UNUM" ("ALL FOR ONE" or "ONE OF MANY") "O"+ "E" = Œ.

Mœris taking the dollar bill with fold made, sees it from the other side, and discovers amazed, that the fold runs right by the eye **œil** of George Washington, and becomes precisely the exact center of the bill and the ox-eye window **œil de bœuf.**

Here, then, something amazing happens: George Washington winks! **clin d'œil** !, as a sign of approval.

Mœris makes his best vows **vœux** for his new company. Now with his little sister **sœurette Clœlia** as partner **consœur Mœris** is going to work **œuvrer** in another way: He will check **jeter un coup d'œil** his actions, change his habits and customs **mœurs** and he will share the secret that was revealed.

Mœris starts his own business that is the creation, distribution and sale of mandalas for wealth and abundance. The first: the mandala of infinite abundance and prosperity, and for suggestion of his little sister **sœurette** always includes another for sharing.

Now, in every transaction, **Mœris** visualises himself and the client, surrounded in a moebius strip **ruban de mœbius** and illuminated by a golden light, in wealth, and infinite abundance, where giving and receiving are fused: like the ligature **Œ.**

The End.

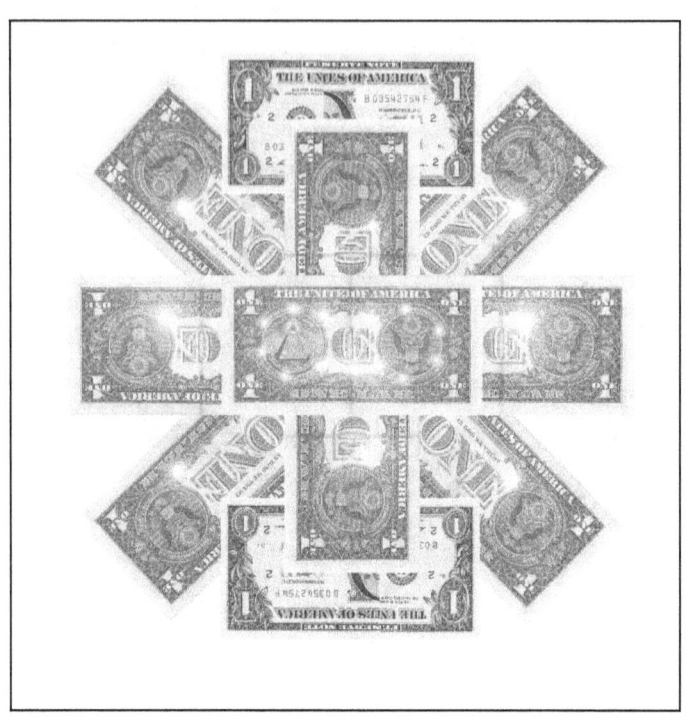

**The mandala of infinite abundance
and prosperity**

ATTACHMENT

To multiply your money
You must share with generosity and infinite
flow like the moebius strip (**Mœbius**)
Without any kind of hard feelings (**Rancœur**)
With all your heart (**Cœur**)
Share because
Giving and receiving is the same
God has favored our company
Our company is successful (**Annuit Cœptis**)
Work (**Œuvrer**) with faith
And
In God We Trust

CLŒLIA

Other works

PUBLICATIONS OF JORGE A RODRIGUEZ
(JAR)
TEXT AND ILLUSTRATIONS:

*MŒRIS AND THE ILLUSTRATED DICTIONARY
OF THE LIGATURE Œ, 2007.
MŒRIS IN THE MUSEUM OF THE LIGATURE
Œ, 2015.*

The mandala of infinite abundance
and prosperity

to SHARE

www.ingramcontent.com/pod-product-compliance
Lightning Source LLC
Chambersburg PA
CBHW071604170526
45166CB00004B/1787